14.95

A SHORT COURSE OF
MEDITATION

SHANTI SADAN

First published in 1993 by Shanti Sadan

Copyright © Shanti Sadan 1993
29 Chepstow Villas
London W11 3DR

*British Library Cataloguing-in-Publication Data.
A catalogue record for this book
is available from the British Library.*

ISBN 0 85424 044 6

*Printed and bound in Great Britain by
WBC Print Ltd, Bridgend*

CONTENTS

LIST OF ILLUSTRATIONS

FOREWORD

Adhyatma Yoga tells us that the final enlightenment (*moksha*), with its concomitants of unbroken inner peace and freedom, is only a new understanding of the world; the scales of mental prejudices and preconceptions drop from our eyes and we see the world in a completely different way, as it really is. Sometimes the Sages refer to this new understanding as awakening from sleep—it is said to be an experience like that. A factor in it is that, by making sincere efforts ourselves with the aid of correct techniques, we attract the Grace of the Lord. The practice of meditation should never be undertaken without a vivid sense of its holy and ultimate purpose of enlightenment.

What exactly is meditation? Hari Prasad Shastri, the Founder of Shanti Sadan, summed it up: 'To meditate means, in the lower stages, to apply thought-force consciously so as to produce harmony within and without, to obtain control over the mind and feelings, and to open up the faculty of intuition . . . In the higher stages, it means the discovery of complete freedom and the finding of God, the *summum bonum*, within one's own self. The normal state of the soul of each individual is what is here described. It is perfection in God. Meditation does not create perfection but allows it to manifest itself by removing obstacles. This is a very important point which must never be ignored'.

This definition implies the progressive nature of meditation, a feature brought out in this short course which was given on Wednesday evenings over six consecutive weeks by a member of Shanti Sadan. The reader who wishes to gain the maximum benefit is advised to follow the same pattern by undertaking the practices in the order given, taking each chapter separately for one week, and devoting at least thirty minutes to them every day over six consecutive weeks.

The instructions are firmly based on the published and unpublished hints of the Founder of Shanti Sadan and of his immediate successor, Marjorie Waterhouse, who has left us many profound insights into the art of meditation in her books *Training the Mind through Yoga* and *The Power Behind the Mind.*

Special thanks are due to Claire Lyth for her artistic help in preparing this little book for publication. Grateful acknowledgement is also made to the Trustees of the British Museum for kindly allowing the use as frontispiece of their photograph of the Japanese carved figure of the Edo period.

WEEK 1: Getting Set Up For Meditation

Reverence to our Teacher, Hari Prasad Shastri!

This is the first Wednesday of a six-week meditation course during which it is proposed to examine the process of meditation stage by stage and to practise a few meditation exercises together.

The only claim which the speaker has to talk to you about this important topic is that he had the privilege of studying for many years under two acknowledged experts in meditation—Hari Prasad Shastri, the Founder of Shanti Sadan, and Marjorie Waterhouse, his immediate successor as Warden of this Centre. Everything you will hear during this course is drawn from the well of their inspiration. Both were great theoreticians who have left an extensive literary legacy on the practice of meditation, and what is important to us is that their theoretical instruction was not derived from reading books or listening to the opinions of others but from their own profound mastery of meditation. Those who came into contact with them felt the power of their meditations to heal and transform, and they were healed and transformed by it.

Look at this picture of another great meditator, Bodhidharma, the Indian monk who took meditation to China. His mind is quiet and collected and his eyes look upwards towards the Universal Truth and not downwards towards the sense-objects. After his famous interview with the Emperor Wu, Bodhidharma spent nine years in meditation in the mountains of Northern China and the power of his meditations transformed the

9

The Sage Bodhidharma

whole art and culture of China and Japan. One of the points made by Zen Master Hakuin is that Bodhidharma had to go to China. Why? Because meditation is a living thing. Otherwise he could have sent a note about meditation to China. A flame has to be lit from a living flame. There are many groups, but traditional centres like Shanti Sadan where the living flame has been received and cherished are few.

In the book *The Heart of the Eastern Mystical Teaching* by Dr Shastri, it is said that 'whether dispensing justice from the royal throne, or instructing the Rishis and Munis in the high wisdom, or fighting on the battlefield, or sporting with the Queens Rukmini and Satyabhama, the Author of the *Gita* was meditating all the time'. The outer and active lives of Dr Shastri and Marjorie Waterhouse were like that too. This is the true mastery of meditation and it is what we have ultimately to aim at. But first we have to start in a small way with some simple basic exercises, which have to be repeated over and over again. However keen one may be to play the piano, one cannot begin by launching immediately into the Hammerklavier Sonata or Rachmaninov's Second Piano Concerto; one has first to acquire technique by practising certain exercises over and over again and starting to play simple pieces. So we shall be doing a few simple meditation exercises during this course but, since the time available is strictly limited, if you want to give these exercises a fair trial and to make real progress in meditation, you will have to practise them at home conscientiously for several weeks before you can have any appreciation of their value. Let me just say again that they are exercises given by experts in meditation: they do work and they will yield their results if done sincerely, conscientiously and in a humble spirit.

We shall begin by listening to Marjorie Waterhouse's advice on how to get set up for meditation:

Before starting to meditate, there are three preliminary things to be established: (1) a rhythm in timing, (2) a rhythm in posture, (3) a rhythm in the preparation to be carried out immediately before the actual meditation begins.

The more conscious a pupil becomes of his inner processes, the more aware he will be of his disharmony, and the more he will strive to correct it. Now in meditation, rhythm is all important. The concentration of thought itself on the actual meditation, and the acts which lead up to that point, should all be carried out in a rhythm; so the pupil must first establish a rhythm in timing. The meditation should be done at the same time every day. It is better to meditate for ten minutes and keep to it, than to allow the time and length of your meditation to change with circumstances. It ought to be the other way round. Just as a fixed time for meals creates a habit and is a helpful factor when the desire for food is weak, so when the mind is disturbed the arrival of the time set apart for meditation may help to turn it in that direction. The digestive juices begin to work in the body as the time for a meal approaches and, in just the same way, the inner urge and sway towards meditation begins to make itself felt as the time set apart for it approaches.

After the rhythm in timing, a rhythm in posture must

be established. In this Yoga we are taught that the establishment of a posture is more important than the actual posture which is selected. The posture must, as far as possible, be independent of exterior things. For example, the floor is preferable to a chair for many reasons, but a strong one is that while you will always have a floor, you may well meet with chairs of different heights and sizes, or no chairs at all. The posture chosen must be able to be held for a long time, for, whatever the pupil may think, his meditation will probably improve in due course, and he will wish to spend more time in it. It is traditional to keep the body motionless and erect, and the eyes either closed or half open. The Lotus posture and others, which are now familiar to the West, can be conquered at the beginning if the body is young enough and strong enough, but the teachers say that provided the posture can be maintained unbroken for as long as necessary, it may be considered as a suitable one. The aim of posture is to accustom the body to a position in which it may be forgotten. Some people will tell you that a posture is held in order to conserve and direct the inner psychic currents of energy in the body. Well, it may be so, but for our purposes it is considered more important to be able to forget the body altogether.

When the pupil has established a rhythm in time and posture, he stands at the threshold of the meditation itself and the preparation that he now makes is very important indeed. Preparation is a ritual, and ritual is a means of arresting the attention and heightening response through the power and attraction of ordered beauty and symbolism. The harmony it produces will be disturbed if it is given excessive importance, but it will probably be absent altogether if it is entirely disregarded.

Having reached this point then, what must our pupil do now? Some will say: 'He must quieten his emotions, concentrate his attention and then start on his meditation'. No! It has been said that the cell of meditation is reached through a very low door, and that anyone who would enter there must bend himself down before he can pass through. The divine Spirit, or the divine Presence, whichever symbol is most in accordance with the heart of the pupil, is *there*, though unseen, and the range and power of spiritual radiation is there also, though undetected as yet by the would-be meditator. He may not feel the spiritual presence or the spiritual power, but he must bow to it in faith all the same, and then, relaxing his hold on outer things, he should turn his inner eye in self-forgetfulness on that which is unseen, and he must rest like this for a short while. In a sense he will be doing what an electrician does with a battery which has run down. He places the battery beside a charged one, connects it and leaves it for a while, and the transfer of power is effected. The pupil places the depleted battery of his mind, emotions and will beside the fully charged battery of the holy truth, connects them by faith, and so remains, relaxed and actionless. He will get to know how long to stay in this condition, and then, having asked for guidance, protection and blessing, he will be fit to enter into meditation.

So there are three preliminaries which have to be got right before entering into meditation: (1) Rhythm in timing, which means doing your meditation at the same time and doing it for a fixed period—whether 5, 10 or 15 minutes—at all events a period which you select and stick to; (2) Rhythm in posture, which means establishing one posture for ᵐeditation which suits you. So far as possible, it should be independent of exterior things. The spine, neck and head should be erect, and the aim is to accustom the body to remain motionless and stable and eventually to be forgotten about; (3) Rhythm in preparation. This is analogous to the rhythmic ritual carried out by a professional golfer before playing a shot. Here it is suggested that before meditating we should feel the presence of the divine Spirit and bow down inwardly to it. A version of this practice was given by St Anselm, the Benedictine monk who became Archbishop of Canterbury in 1093 AD:

OM

Flee thy occupation. Cast aside thy burdensome cares and put away thy toilsome business. Hide thyself from thy disturbing thoughts. Yield room to God and rest for a little time in Him. Enter the inner chamber of thy mind. Shut out all thought save that of God. Close thy door and seek Him.

OM

The practice which we have just done, as well as reminding us that we are in the presence of God, is an aid to stilling the mind. Our Teacher once defined meditation as 'the continual uninterrupted reflection on the Truth in the silence of the mind'. Getting set up for meditation means above all stilling the mind, and so we will now attempt a practice designed for this purpose and given by Marjorie Waterhouse. These are her words

15

to describe it:

> Sit either on the floor or upright but not rigid on a chair. Make a mental salutation either to an Incarnation of God or to the abstract all-pervading Spirit, and breathe in and out for a few minutes, bringing in the breath as from the feet to the head, and releasing it as from the head to the feet. Imagine that this breath has the power to dissolve all thought, as a light wind dissolves a mist. When you feel that the mind is still—or stiller than it was—cease the breathing and remain quiet yet alert for a short time. Then place one chosen sentence in the mind and look at it and absorb it.

The sentence which we will choose on this occasion is: 'I sit in the direct light and stillness of Thy being'. The thought is that we are sitting in the presence of God and our being is bathed in the light and stillness of His being. So, to recapitulate the practice:

OM

Mental salutation to God in personal or impersonal form.
Deep breathing from feet to head and from head to feet, imagining that the breath is dissolving all thought.
Short pause in silence.
Then place in the mind and concentrate on the thought (which is a fact): 'OM. I sit in the direct light and stillness of Thy being'.

OM

The second practice, which follows on—both are to

16

be found in the book *The Power Behind the Mind*—is described in these words:

> The second practice is the one which opens the heart to the universality of Consciousness or God and the consequent oneness of all. Sit still in the posture, but now your mind must be ready to receive thought. You say to it: 'May all derive good from me. May I derive good from all.' Meditate on the thought for about five minutes. You will notice that the idea has two stages: 'May all derive good from me' and 'May I derive good from all.' The second part of the thought is inserted to prevent the Lord of the Manor attitude from developing in the pupil! The sense of being a universal benefactor and the subtle satisfaction this procedure produces spells a temporary victory for the ego and must be avoided at all costs, and this is a sure way to do it.

In the recommended posture, sitting still and composed, let us do this practice for a few minutes. The thought is:

OM

May all derive good from me.
May I derive good from all.

OM

In relation to these two practices, Marjorie Waterhouse says:

> No doubt these practices will look as if they are very childish and easy, but this is not always found to be the

case when they are tried out. You will only get to know how wiry your mind is when you try to quieten it and make it supple for even a few minutes . . . If the practices do begin to have a result, which should take the form of a sense of security, peace and expansion, then you can go forward into the practice of meditation with a hopeful heart. May this be so.

We have made a start this week in taking practical steps to create silence in the mind, in the context of Dr Shastri's definition of meditation as 'the continued uninterrupted reflection on the Truth in the silence of the mind'. In the meditation period we try for a short while to cast off from the shore of sense impressions and ego experiences and sail in silence on the infinite sea of Truth. We will end with a short poem written by a Japanese lady in the 11th century which refers to this:

> I yearn for a tranquil moment
> To be out upon the sea of harmony
> In that enchanted boat.
> O boatman, do you know my heart?

WEEK 2: Bringing the Mind under Control

Reverence to the Founder of Shanti Sadan, Hari Prasad Shastri, and to his successor as Warden, Marjorie Waterhouse!

The aspect of meditation which we shall be concentrating upon this week is bringing the mind under control. But we will begin by repeating the practice which we did last week and which is designed to make the mind still and also to remind us that in meditation we are sitting in the presence of a higher power which you can call the Supreme Spirit or God or Christ or Buddha—the name chosen is not important:

Sit either on the floor or upright but not rigid on a chair. Make a mental salutation either to an Incarnation of God or to the abstract all-pervading Spirit, and breathe in and out for a few minutes, bringing in the breath as from the feet to the head, and releasing it as from the head to the feet. Imagine that this breath has the power to dissolve all thought, as a light wind dissolves a mist. When you feel that the mind is still—or stiller than it was—cease the breathing and remain quiet yet alert for a short time. Then place in the mind the sentence: 'OM. I sit in the direct light and stillness of Thy being'. Look at it with your mind's eye and absorb it. So the steps in order are:

OM

Mental salutation to God in personal or impersonal form.
Deep breathing from feet to head and from head to feet, imagining that the breath is dissolving all thought. Short pause in silence.

19

Then place in the mind and concentrate on: 'OM. I sit in the direct light and stillness of Thy being'.

OM

Ox and Rider

It is an axiom of Yoga that your mind can be your worst enemy and also your best friend. When it is uncontrolled, it is a constant source of suffering and keeps you in bondage. A popular tune of the 1930s with a neat lyric was 'The trouble with me is you'; it applies to the uncontrolled mind. And yet it is the mind, when controlled, which is the key to God-Realization. This is the theme of the well-known ox-herding pictures of China and Japan. The ox has first to be located, then it has to be brought under control—a process which requires skill, courage and perseverance—until (as in this picture) the herdsman has asserted such mastery that he can ride unconcernedly on the back of the ox. Marjorie Waterhouse tells us: 'The idea which lies behind training is the shifting of the mastery of the personality from the instruments to the owner of them, and the consequent awakening in him of his divinity, power and independence'. Our main instrument is the mind, and so often it is the mind that calls the tune. The object of training is that the ox of the mind is no longer to be allowed to wander about wherever it will, dragging us this way and that, but is to become an obedient servant to carry out our purposes; this is an essential stage on the way to God-Realization.

It is necessary first to understand exactly what we are trying to do. The very first step is to disidentify yourself from the mind, to see it as something objective. The mind is like the ox: you are the rider and you are different from the ox. Then the second step is gaining control. Control can be exercised much better if one is not identified with what has to be controlled.

Statuette of Ox and Rider

But let us hear, in an extended passage, what Marjorie Waterhouse has to say about this:

On the principle that it is always easier to deal in a detached way with other people's troubles than with your own, the first item of training is to disentangle and disidentify yourself from your mind, to look on it as if it were your pupil and then to direct it from a distance. In order to achieve this disidentification, you must affirm again and again, until it becomes a sort of mantram to you, that you are not the body, that you are not the mind, but that you are superior to them—that you are the supreme spirit. Having reiterated this for some time, you change the affirmation to: 'The mind is my instrument. I, the supreme Power, can and will control it'. Having spent some time on this, and only you will know how long it should be, you start the next practice, which is carrying out what you have affirmed—the controlling of the instrument.

It is inevitable that these practices will appear baby-easy at first, but it is also inevitable that most people will find them quite enough to employ them for some time. To control the mind you must learn to start it, steer it and stop it, as if it were a car. The aim of this trio of practices—starting, steering and stopping—is to bring the mind into focus as an object, and then to teach it to obey your orders. If you do not become at any rate partially successful in these preliminary practices, your later experiences in meditation and conscious living will somewhat resemble surf-bathing, or being on the witching waves at a fair.

You can do the exercises given at any time. In fact, it is almost better to do them in the day, during your working life, than when shut up by yourself in your room. For instance, as you are sitting in the train, going to work and reading the daily paper, give your mind the order: 'Stop!', and instantly cease reading, and not only cease reading, but make your mind cease to think of what it has been reading. Hold it in suspension for a minute and then start it again on an entirely different theme.

It doesn't matter at this stage whether the subject you now present it with is secular or spiritual. The purpose of the practice is to teach your mind obedience, Say you decide to think for five minutes about your summer holiday, or about your coming work during the day, or about the meaning of a sentence you read earlier in a spiritual classic—it is all one. Let the mind carry out the order and then stop it again when the time limit has been reached. In this way you are practising starting, steering and stopping the mind.

These practices must seem almost inane and very restricting, but they will not have to be used for long. After a certain time, varying with each pupil, the mind will have learnt to obey a percentage, at any rate, of your orders, or alternatively, you will be aware of its disobedience. In either case you will have brought your mind into focus. These practices should never be persisted in for very long at a time. The mind must be given frequent rests. The control will become automatic in due course, as the dancing steps become automatic after the agony of the first lesson is over.

This control lays the foundation on which meditation and consciously directed action are based. Control is imperative, for a mind which is capable of sustained concentration only when it is interested, and which refuses to apply itself to anything which is foreign and distasteful to it, will be of no use to you when you get to the higher reaches of Yoga.

Practise moderation: that is, get to know how long you can stand these exercises before you get tired of them and dismiss them as no good. Great things very often start in small ways, and if you persevere with these suggestions, you will have cause to be thankful all your yogic life.

Just to get some idea of the double practice suggested by Marjorie Waterhouse, we will try each part separately for a few minutes. As she says, they are relatively easy, and everyone should be able to manage them without difficulty:

OM

For two minutes repeat, and go on repeating interiorly: 'I am not the body, I am not the mind. I am the supreme spirit'.

OM

OM

Now, this time for three minutes, change the affirmation and go on repeating interiorly: 'The mind is my instrument. I, the supreme Power, can and will control it'.

OM

A very important point, which is probably becoming clear to you, is that control of the mind—and therefore meditation itself—can only be brought about if the mind is kept on a tight rein throughout the day. Listen again to what our expert has to say:

Now, if the pupil looks on meditation as an isolated act which he must carry out at certain times, and which calls mainly for concentration and obedience on his part,

25

he will remain for a long time in the kindergarten, for unless he takes advantage of the opportunities which come to him during the day, and learns to use them in order to control and direct his mind, he will not accustom it to be obedient; and so when the time comes for meditation, he will not be able to give it orders—or rather, he may give it orders, but it will not obey them. Provided it is lived consciously, the day offers the best preparation for meditation, and the time for meditation provides the best preparation for the activities of the day.

The efforts of our own will to control the mind have to be exerted, but it is also most helpful to pray for assistance from God, the supreme Spirit and the Source of all power. A charming example of this is the prayer of a nun in the 17th century (see opposite page), although naturally our own prayer would be couched in our own terms.

'Constructive living can only be attained when the pupil has learned to live *in* his body and mind and not *as* his body and mind'. This phrase of Marjorie Waterhouse sums up the essence of disidentifying from the mind. You have to live in the body and mind as a guest or a lodger, she says. Her double practice, which we did earlier, is a practical method of (1) disidentifying oneself from the mind and (2) creating the framework for controlling it. Do it during the week.

We will now move on to a further practice for which she suggests a precise method:

LORD Thou knowest better than I know myself that I am growing older and will some day be old. Keep me from the fatal habit of thinking I must say something on every subject and on every occasion. Release me from craving to straighten out everybody's affairs. Make me thoughtful but not moody: helpful but not bossy. With my vast store of wisdom, it seems a pity not to use it all, but Thou knowest Lord that I want a few friends at the end.

Keep my mind free from the recital of endless details; give me wings to get to the point. Seal my lips on my aches and pains. They are increasing, and love of rehearsing them is becoming sweeter as the years go by. I dare not ask for grace enough to enjoy the tales of others' pains, but help me to endure them with patience.

I dare not ask for improved memory, but for a growing humility and a lessing cocksureness when my memory seems to clash with the memories of others. Teach me the glorious lesson that occasionally I may be mistaken.

Keep me reasonably sweet; I do not want to be a Saint - some of them are so hard to live with - but a sour old person is one of the crowning works of the devil. Give me the ability to see good things in unexpected places, and talents in unexpected people. And, give me, O Lord, the grace to tell them so. AMEN

Five minutes is a minimum, but if you can manage longer and can keep to it, it will be all to the good ... It is a good practice in will-power. Remind yourself again and again that as the Lord is omnipresent, you are doing this meditation in His presence. The meditation is: 'Show Thy Face to me. Make me worthy of Thy love, O Love Supreme, O Beauty Absolute'. This is a prayer to the Unconditioned, asking that It may become conditioned. When you have repeated it a few times, then gather up the central meaning in your heart as, so to say, 'reveal, reveal!' and feel and contemplate it there. Then wait, in a quiescent receptive state—not for a vision of that Face but for a sense of its reality and immanence.

We will do it for five minutes. Remind yourself you are in His presence, then repeat the text and *feel* 'reveal, reveal!' Then wait for the revelation which will come in some form:

OM

Show Thy Face to me. Make me worthy of Thy love, O Love Supreme, O Beauty Absolute.

OM

Finally, here is a practice which may be done during the day, and which could easily turn out to be the most valuable of all in bringing the mind under control. Again it is given in Marjorie Waterhouse's own words, and she recommends: 'Do not try to do this all day, because if you do you will probably pass judgment against it and forget all about it. Do it for, say, half an hour at a time, and repeat the practice at definite times during the day':

28

OM

Remember that you are performing action and undergoing all experience in the invisible presence of the Lord, and look upon all that comes as a message from Him to you, and on your reaction to it as an offering from you to Him.

OM

We will end with a short poem by the Japanese poet Mumon:

Hundreds of spring flowers, the autumnal moon,
A refreshing summer breeze, winter snow—
Free thy mind from idle thoughts
And for thee how enjoyable is every season!

Sengai In Meditation

WEEK 3: Feeling the Meditation

Reverence to our Teacher, Hari Prasad Shastri!

The two pictures to look at today are of figures sitting in meditation which, in their separate ways, exemplify the qualities required in meditation. The picture on page 30 is of Sengai, the Abbot of a famous Zen monastery in Japan and a celebrated artist: he lived from 1750 to 1837. When Gautama sat down under the Bo-tree, he vowed he would not get up until he had attained enlightenment. Determination—you can see it in the face of Sengai. Great determination is needed to bring the mind under control, which was our theme last week.

The Japanese carved figure (page 32)—you can see how calm he is. Meditation has to be started with a calm mind, which was the theme of our first session. Calm and patient. Impatience in meditation spoils everything (either impatience with the mind or impatience with lack of quick results). There is a folksong of Bali: 'The stars, the sun and the moon are never impatient. Silently they float along the stream of pure Existence'.

By looking at such pictures we can begin to get the feel of meditation. Meditation is the key which can unlock the door beyond which lies eternal peace and bliss. The lock is not an entirely straightforward one—Maya has seen to that!—and the hand has to be taught how to turn the key. The hand that turns the key is the mind (which includes the will). The trained mind, using the key of meditation, can unlock the door beyond which lies eternal peace and bliss.

Keeping Calm

As we have already seen, the first requirement is that the hand should be empty. Unless the hand is empty, it will not be able to hold the key properly or to manipulate it in the lock. The key itself cannot make the hand empty; that is to say, meditation of itself cannot make the mind empty. That is why the yogic discipline of vairagya has to be practised assiduously during the day. Vairagya means avoiding attachment to persons or objects and gradually freeing the mind from binding desires, including the latent desires deep in the sub-conscious known as vasanas. It is no use at all sitting down and expecting to practise meditation successfully unless effective efforts to increase vairagya are made during the day. Otherwise a plethora of desires, ideas and worries will re-appear in the mind at the time of meditation and produce agitation and distraction.

A wise saying of Marjorie Waterhouse is: 'In order to become detached from anything, the mind must be convinced that it can obtain greater satisfaction elsewhere'. This thought goes to the root of the practice with which we will begin and which we have previously done. In doing it, we put aside for the time being all the petty considerations of our daily life and envisage ourselves—and it is a fact whether we realize it or not—sitting in the presence of God and being embraced by the light of His being. The method is:

OM

Mental salutation to God in either personal or impersonal form.
Deep breathing from feet to head and from head to

feet, imagining that the breath is dissolving all thought.
Short pause in silence.
Then place the following thought in the mind and feel
it as vividly as you can: 'OM. I sit in the direct light
and stillness of Thy being'.

OM

Another important statement from Marjorie Water-house is: 'All spiritual training, whether yogic or otherwise, has for its aim the withdrawal of the mental or Mayic activity to the background in order that this divine Power may manifest, may be brought to the fore-ground and finally dominate the scene'. It is through meditation that the mind can get at first a glimpse, and later on flashes, of something far more satisfying and productive of far greater bliss than anything experienced through the senses. When the mind realizes that its real home is in the One, that its supreme satisfaction lies there, it does not need to be told to turn away from sense-satisfaction; it will naturally abandon it in favour of the greater satisfaction.

If, with the help of the daily discipline of vairagya, we can learn to withdraw from the orbit of sense-objects at the time of meditation, we can make use of that very force which has been drawing us towards them. Freud maintains that the life-force and the love-force are one and the same. When the love-force goes outwards to the sense-objects it is called 'desire' and the mind is agitated. Far from wanting to stifle this love-force—even if we were able to do it, which we are not—we want to harness it in the service of meditation, because it is perhaps the most valuable asset we possess. What we have to do is to redirect this love-force to the spiritual Truth within ourselves, knowing that we will discover greater satisfaction there. This is what is called 'feeling the meditation'.

To quote Marjorie Waterhouse again: 'Love is the quickest and surest way to gain intensity, whether in the outer or inner world; therefore the teachers train their disciples to love. But love according to the yogic terminology has nothing necessarily to do with emotion: it is an inner conviction and recognition of basic identity with an individual or a concept and the consequent desire to unite with it'. It is the love-force which initially gives intensity to our meditation.

Before doing the next practice we will listen to a poem—perhaps more a prayer than a poem—by our Teacher. Such prayers or poems can be chosen and read before doing our meditations and often help to intensify the feeling we will want to bring to the practice:

O Omniscient Bliss! O Creator of heaven and earth! Our minds have their roots in Thee, as the rivers have their source in the high glaciers. Wandering through the hills of reason, the flowery fields of emotions, the rocky soil of asceticism, the wind-swept valleys of scepticism, they must, O Hari, finally unite themselves with Thee, through devotion to truth and service of Thy children.

May we ever remember, O Spirit of shanti, that Thou art the only goal of our life, the sole garden of peace for our fatigued feet and restless minds.

Pour Thy light into our hearts in the form of viveka and vairagya, so that we may resolutely fight against the obstacles of pleasure-desire, pride, vanity, egoity and meanness of the heart.

May we love the poor, the mourning, the oppressed and the sick and restore in them the balance of the mind.

Like the cuckoo, singing unseen in the spring, may we chant adorations to Thee, from the leafy branches of humility: 'Thou art One, the only Reality'.

Now the practice, which is a repetition of the one we did last week and which Marjorie Waterhouse explains in these words:

Remind yourself again and again that, as the Lord is omnipresent, you are doing this meditation in His presence. The meditation is: 'Show Thy Face to me. Make me worthy of Thy love, O Love Supreme, O Beauty Absolute'. This is a prayer to the Unconditioned, asking that It may become conditioned. When you have repeated it a few times, then gather up the central meaning in your heart as, so to say, 'reveal, reveal!' and feel and contemplate it there. Then wait, in a quiescent receptive state—not for a vision of that Face but for a sense of its reality and immanence.

I will repeat the text once more and we will do it for five minutes, imagining, as we offer the words, that we are in the actual presence of the Lord:

OM

Show Thy Face to me. Make me worthy of Thy
love, O Love Supreme, O Beauty Absolute.

OM

For the last practice today, we will take a new
meditation text. But first we will listen to the passage in
which the Mahatma Swami Rama Tirtha introduces it in
his own words. Notice particularly the emphasis which
he puts on feeling the meditation:

This is a form of prayer. It is not a prayer in the sense
that it begs, asks or seeks anything from God. It is a
prayer in this sense, that it enables you to realize your
divinity. Sit at your ease . . . You may close your eyes,
begin in a prayerful mood, or keep your eyes half closed,
just as you wish. Then say: 'There is but one reality. OM!
OM! OM! There is but one reality'. You know that that
is the truth. All those who have taken interest in Rama's
lectures know that that is the truth, and when you are
convinced that that is the truth, feel it. 'There is but one
reality'. Say that in the language of feeling, say that with
your whole heart; melt in the idea: 'There is but one
reality. OM! OM! OM!'

Now see that after this verse, 'There is but one
reality', there is written opposite to it, 'OM! OM! OM!'
What does that signify? That signifies that when you have
filled your heart and saturated your mind with the idea
that there is but one reality, instead of reading out all
these words, one, two, three, four, five, say only one
word, 'OM', as this word represents the whole idea to
you. In algebra, we represent big quantities by x or y, a or

b or some other letter. Just so, when you have read out this thought 'There is but one reality', this name 'OM', which is the holy of holies, this name OM, possessing the highest powers of divinity or God, should be chanted, and while chanting it feel the idea that there is but one reality. While your lips are chanting 'OM', your whole soul should feel the idea that there is but one reality.

At present, to you the words 'There is but one reality' are most probably mere jargon; they convey no sense to you. But if you have heard Rama's lectures, you must know that there is but one reality. It ought to have a concrete meaning for you. It means that all this phenomenal universe, which dampens our spirit and mars our joy, all this phenomenal universe of difference, is no reality; the reality is only one—all the circumstances are no reality. This is the meaning. Those who have not tried this experiment and have frittered away their energies alone deny the existence of this one reality. It is just as much a matter of experience as any experiment performed in any laboratory; it is a solid stern fact. When you melt your mind, when you lose your little false self in the divinity, what is the consequence? The consequence is (mark the words of Jesus of Nazareth) that if you have a mustard seed's worth of faith and bid the mountain to come, it will come. Live that reality; feel that reality, and you will see that all your circumstances, all your imminent dangers, all the troubles and anxieties that stare you in the face, are bound to disappear.

You put more faith in the outside phenomena than in the divinity; you make the world more real than God. You have hypnotized yourself into a rigidity with regard to outside phenomena, and thus it is that you involve yourself in all sorts of sickness and trouble. Take up this affirmation whenever you are much dejected, and feel that there is but one reality. See that this one statement is a higher statement than all the so-called truths insinuated in you through the books. All the so-called facts which you believe are simply an illusion, a delusion hypnotized into you by the senses. Be not dupes of the senses. Somebody comes and finds fault with you and criticizes you; another comes and abuses you; another comes and puffs you up and flatters you. All these are not facts; all these are not reality. You should feel the reality, the stern fact. When chanting this, drive out and expel all the beliefs that you have put into the outside phenomenal circumstances. Put forth all your energies and strength on this fact: 'There is but one reality'. Feel that. 'There is but one reality. OM! OM! OM!'

So let us soak our minds in the truth of these words, in the manner explained by Swami Rama Tirtha:

OM

There is but one reality. OM! OM! OM!

OM

Patanjali says in one of his aphorisms that the goal of meditation is closest to the one who is most ardent and puts all he has into the meditation. Marjorie Waterhouse is making the same point in these words: 'How long meditation remains in the preliminary stage is dependent, before anything else, on the devotion and imagination the beginner brings to it. By 'devotion' I mean the attention he will give to it, the sacrifices he will offer it, and the efforts he will make to live according to his meditation during the day. By 'imagination' I mean the capacity and will to believe that what he is meditating on is not a mere theoretical formula but a living truth and, most important of all, that it applies to him personally'. This all points to the importance of this week's theme, that of feeling the meditation.

Next week we shall progress to another practical point, that of creating the focus, but I will leave you this week by reminding you of the practice recommended to be done at definite times of the day and for a period of not longer than half an hour in the initial stages:

OM

Remember that you are performing action and undergoing all experience in the invisible presence of the Lord, and look upon all that comes as a message from Him to you, and on your reaction to it as an offering from you to Him'.

OM

We will end with a few lines from John Clare's poem 'I am':

I long for scenes where man hath never trod,
A place where woman never smiled or wept,
There to abide with my Creator, God,
And sleep as I in childhood sweetly slept;
Untroubling and untroubled where I lie
The grass below—above, the vaulted sky.

WEEK 4: Creating the Focus

Reverence to Hari Prasad Shastri and to Marjorie Water-house, both of whom have shed so much light on the difficult art of meditation!

In a lecture which he gave on the 4th November 1954, our Teacher said that 'to meditate means to focus the mind one-pointedly, restraining the five senses and focussing it on something which is abstract in your mind. This is called meditation. By doing so, your mind becomes saturated in what you meditate upon and afterwards it reproduces the same in your conduct'.

This deceptively simple statement of a profound truth which goes to the very heart of meditation is elaborated by Marjorie Waterhouse in a short passage:

The training which Adhyatma Yoga offers consists of a process whereby an enquirer, having followed certain disciplines, succeeds in diverting his concentrated attention from the outer to the inner world. This makes it possible, in course of time, for a focus to be set up within him which will claim his love and service. After further instruction and meditation, such a focus, which can be an abstract concept or an inner visualization, does arise within him, and he concentrates and meditates upon it. Later on, this focus loses its objective character and is recognised by the pupil as one with the Power residing within him, as his own Self—his centre. Finally, through the ultimate revelations of the philosophy, and his now intuitive understanding, he realises that this centre of Consciousness is not only within himself, but that it is the supreme reality or Truth—revealed to his awakened inner sense as all-pervading, the same within as without, and absolute.

Henceforth, whatever action he performs or whatever situation he finds himself in, he experiences no change in consciousness, for he is centred in this supreme and universal spirit—he is one with it. This transition, from focussed consciousness to being, is a transition which must be made by every serious follower of this Yoga, for it brings about the transition from dependence to freedom.

This is our main topic this evening—how to create a focus within us which will claim our love and service, after having first directed our concentrated attention from the outer to the inner world.

This focus will initially have to be either an inner visualization or an intuitive feeling of our Universal Self, which is called Atman in Sanskrit. Shankara refers to it in his commentary on the *Bhagavad Gita* 18.55: 'The devotion of knowledge (jnana-nishtha) consists in an intent effort to establish a continuous current of the idea of the Inner Self (Pratyagatman)'.

Take this scroll, which represents the Universal Self as the moon and the objects of the world as the bamboo branches. The moon is very very faint, hardly to be seen, despite the fact that if we were present at the scene it would be by its light, and only by its light, that we would be able to see the bamboos at all. On the other hand, the bamboos thrust themselves on our attention in the foreground. The founder of Hasidic Judaism said: 'Exile is caused by forgetfulness, and the secret of redemption

Moon and Bamboos

is remembering'. Our spiritual exile is caused by forget-fulness of the Moon.

Our task is to withdraw our attention from the foreground and to shift the focus to the background and, in doing this, we can take advantage of one of the psychological peculiarities of the mind, namely that it can only concentrate on one thing at a time.

This diagram may help to make the point clearer. One of the axioms of the Gestalt theory of perception is that we cannot be aware of any *image* except in relation to a *ground*. In this diagram you *either* see two people looking at each other against a black ground *or* a chalice standing against a white ground. Your mind will not see both at once, In fact the mind *sees* by concentrating on and interpreting an image—e.g. the chalice—and ignor-ing the ground.

Yoga says that this is what is happening to us. The Ground of all our experiences is Self or God (the Moon and its light) but we ignore It and focus exclusively on the images presented by our five senses, by memory and imagination—in other words the bamboo branches in the foreground. The crucial step for meditation is to stop focussing on the bamboos and to set up the inner focus of the Moon. If this can be done, we are assured by Marjorie Waterhouse, we shall slowly become more aware of the Moon of Self and of the descent and interpenetration of its light into the mind—and in fact less and less will go on in the mind under that influence.

This important process can be initiated by the simple

The Chalice

practices which we have already tried earlier in the course and which we will repeat now:

OM

For two minutes repeat and go on repeating interiorly: 'I am not the body, I am not the mind, I am the supreme spirit'.

OM

(This is to disidentify from the bamboos)

OM

Again for two minutes, change the affirmation and go on repeating interiorly: 'The mind is my instrument. I, the supreme power, can and will control it'.

OM

(This is to set up the inner focus of the Moon of Self)

Now, before doing the next practice to set up the focus, let us first listen to a further short passage from Marjorie Waterhouse about the technique of focussing:

Meditation is the most potent means that exists for learning how to centre the mind. By its practice the mind learns to accept an idea or an object, and then to fasten itself upon it, entering deeper and deeper into it, until its underlying nature is sensed. Now this may seem very advanced, but these recognitions can be experienced in miniature even by a beginner. Some think that a practice will have no result until it has been perfected, but this is not so. A baby grows from the first moment it takes its first drink, and what is more, it learns to associate that drink with well-being and looks forward to it. So it is with the beginner in meditation. Truths begin to dawn upon him from the start.

Meditation is rather like getting a camera into focus before taking a picture—a proper picture—a time exposure, not a snap! Endless concentrated experiment and movement are necessary to arrive at the proper distance from the object and to get the picture in the view-finder. When the camera is at last focussed, a new state of things begins. Now there must be no more experiment and no more movement if the picture is to be successfully impressed on the film of the mind, and many under-exposures have to be discarded before even a passable photograph is obtained.

No sooner has the mental camera been focussed, than the state of contemplation begins. At first this manifests as the realization of a *capacity*—no more than that—but later, when it can be sustained, contemplation will be known as the process by which the picture is taken.

Now let us take positive action with our own mental camera to create the focus by *feeling* the meditation we did last week:

OM

There is but one reality. OM! OM! OM!

OM

Feeling the meditation we have just done has two definite effects, which may be illustrated by these two diagrams:

Diagram 1

Diagram 2

(1) We begin to become much more aware of that One Reality which is the Ground of all our experience, and it emerges as a focus like the three bands of the black ground which are emphasized in Diagram 2.

(2) The second effect is that the objects of the world acquire a unity which they have not had before; they seem to be all part of one pattern. In Diagram 1 the figures look distinct and unconnected, whereas in Diagram 2 they form part of one meaningful whole.

In working to create the focus, it is useful to reinforce the meditation by reading passages of prose or poetry which expound the same truth. This may be done before or after the meditation, or at a convenient moment during the day. As an example of this, following the meditation practice which we have just done, we will listen to a poem by Nazir, a famous Sufi poet of Agra who died in the year 1820 at the age of 80 and who was much admired by the Mahatma Swami Rama Tirtha and by our Teacher, who translated this poem from the original Urdu:

O Soul, do not move thy lips to beg a favour from
    anybody;
Do not expose the pain of thy heart to anyone;
Approach Him who can satisfy thy ambitions for ever.
There is a famous proverb; I presume thou knowest it:
'Except God, none has the power to confer a favour on
    anybody'.

All are powerless before Him; He dispenses gifts and
    causes them to be bestowed;

He is the ruler and creator of the world, He is the
    governor and He the wise.
He confers favours, He is the Ancient, and the
    compassionate One;
He is verily the pardoner, He is the beneficent One;
'Except God, none has the power to confer a favour on
    anybody'.

He is the home of glory and majesty, He is the sole Lord
    of nature;
He confers the wherewithal and protection; He is the
    helper and the friend.
The man, the god, the genii, the houris, the camel, the
    ant, the snake,
All these are supported by His hand alone.
'Except God, none has the power to confer a favour on
    anybody'.

Give up dependence on the rich of this world;
Do not flatter others, do not cringe before them.
Turn thy hands away from those who have two hands;
Ask favours of Him who has millions of hands.
'Except God, none has the power to confer a favour on
    anybody'.

Ask Him for wealth, silver, rubies, pearls;
Ask Him for boxes, property, packages and bundles.
If thou dost desire a son, go and ask of Him.
However small thy want, make it known to Him, and to
    none else.
'Except God, none has the power to confer a favour on
    anybody'.

If thou art in His favour, then thy enemy will shower
    favours on thee;
If He is against thee, even thy oldest bosom friends will
    forsake thee.
Without His permission, even a slice of bread shalt thou
    not receive;
A glassful of water too will they deny thee, unless He be
    thy friend.
'Except God, none has the power to confer a favour on
    anybody'.

The officials, the men of eminence, the king and the
    vizier,
God alone is their patron; in themselves they are beggars.
Wealth, territory, home, crown and majesty, ask of Him,
He is the sole bestower of favours.
O good Nazir: 'Except God, none has the power to
    confer a favour on anybody'.

Our last practice today will be a simplified version of
one we have done previously and about which Marjorie
Waterhouse has said that 'after you have practised it
with visual imagination for a certain time, it settles itself
as a background to the activities of your mind'. In other
words you will have created a focus. The practice is to
concentrate and feel as vividly as you can: 'I sit in the
direct light and stillness of Thy being'.

OM

I sit in the direct light and stillness of Thy being.

OM

The significance of what we have just been doing is lucidly summarized in the words of Marjorie Waterhouse:

> An intensely held and visualized inner thought or picture is infinite in its range and power. The creative power of a focus is realized by few, but to produce and maintain such a focus is the highest sacrifice that an individual can offer to the whole, involving a process of selection and rejection, and the capacity for continuity of effort. After a while, the disciple's focus on the spiritual power, and on its source, does not need to be the subject of constant active thought, but it must form the background for all activity; for all action, mental and physical, must be carried out in front of it. This sacrifice will not become a part of the nature until repeated dedications in meditation have been made.

We will end with a short Japanese haiku, which refers to the successful creation of a spiritual focus:

> O joy! To rise and find by morning's ray
> A flower which was not there yesterday.

The Circle of Creation

WEEK 5: Self-Identification

Reverence to Hari Prasad Shastri!

The speaker once heard a lady in a bus comforting her companion by saying: 'Be philosophical, my dear: don't think about it'. Whether this is a useful definition of philosophy or not is for others to say. Our Teacher has said: 'Real knowledge is forgetting. In meditation you have to forget body and mind, life, home, all. What remains? He who forgets'.

It is an important clue to what the *Bhagavad Gita* means in Chapter 13 where it says: 'By dhyana (meditation) they see the Self'. The jewel of Self is in the lotus of the mind but it is hidden under the innumerable petals of the lotus, i.e., the vrittis or movements of the mind. If by some means or other we can forget all the vrittis in meditation, we can have the real knowledge of the Self. The words of our Teacher are: 'The process of meditation affects our whole being. First, by exercise of the will, we create an inner silence and then put the text of the meditation on it. When a mental state is attained in which the subjective consciousness is merged in meditation and there is no such feeling as 'I am meditating', the whole being is flooded with spiritual peace (shanti) and the hidden jewel of Self is seen'.

This is the phase of meditation which is to be considered this evening and which may be termed 'Self-identification'. It is the phase which, in the famous ox-herding pictures, is represented by a blank circle, somewhat similar to this scroll. The Chinese ox-herding pictures are traditionally drawn in a circle. The circle resembles one of the Chinese circular polished mirrors, and the idea is that in a polished mirror of this type the whole process of meditation from start to finish—from the beginnings of quietening and controlling the mind to the end of Self-Knowledge or God-Realization—is reflected stage by stage. Of course, the reference is to an inner mirror, not an outer one.

One of the stages depicts a blank circle, but it is not the final stage because the one who has fully mastered samadhi comes back, so to say, into the world of time, space and causation, this time riding unconcernedly on the ox of the mind. There he acts and teaches for the benefit of society, and his whole life is a continuous meditation. This explains why, in this picture, the blank circle has a blurry mark on the top edge; it signifies that, for such an illumined man, there is still a slight awareness of the world of duality, even though he is ever fixed on the One Reality.

Returning now to the phase of Self-identification, which is our topic this evening, let us first hear one of the traditional Chinese poems descriptive of the stage of the blank circle in the ox-herding pictures:

> Whip and rein, ox and herdsman—all vanished
> without trace.
> In the vast blue sky, words can never suffice to
> measure It.
> How could snow survive in the red flame of the
> burning fire?
> Only when one has succeeded in reaching this
> place can he match the old Sages.

With one blow, the vast sky is suddenly shattered
    into pieces.
'Holy' and 'worldly' have both vanished without
    trace.
Where none can tread, ends the way.
The bright moon shines and the wind rustles in
    front of the temple.
All waters of all rivers flow into the great sea.

It is a description of the indescribable. No one can hope to undertake the advanced meditation practices for reaching this stage until his mind is so quietened and controlled that he can meditate one-pointedly for an hour or so, but we can usefully discuss this stage and advance towards it by doing simpler practices for a shorter time to begin with.

Meditation is a serious business. It is not a parlour game, and not for the weak-willed. It is very difficult and requires great courage and patience and perseverance, but the prize is great. Bodhidharma, who first took meditation to the Far East from India in the sixth century AD, is said to have meditated for nine years facing the wall of a temple in Northern China. It was a blank wall, without any forms on it, strong and unmoving. Among other things, this tradition indicates that our mind has to become like that wall before the final transformations can take place.

Therefore, making our mind like that wall, let us meditate in silence for five minutes on the text:

OM

There is but one reality. OM! OM! OM!

OM

Now it is time to turn to our expert guide in
meditation, Marjorie Waterhouse, and to hear what she
has to say about the three stages of meditation and the
phase of Self-identification which is their culmination:

During the first stage, the text is thought about word
by word and sentence by sentence, rather in the way a
lawyer reads a document. Then, when the mind has
become imbued with the outer meaning of the words, the
next stage begins. Now the mind and reason take a
second place, and the imagination and intuition are
brought into play. The fact which is the central point of
the meditation is now encompassed by the imagination,
and its truth intuitively recognised. The content of the
meditation is now *experienced*, rather than understood by
the mind. This produces a growing and a deepening
attention and should be held for as long as possible.

The third stage is the culmination of the actual
meditation. At a certain point, the mind, imagination and
the intuitive faculty go into abeyance, or rather they
remain in a state of suspension, rather like a hawk
hovering *apparently* motionless, above its prey. No
perceptible motion of the wings, only an alert regard
from above on the prey—the text—below. The pupil
must teach himself to believe—and it is a literal
fact—that this is the seed time of the meditation, the
time when the truth of the affirmation, which has already

been thought upon and intuitively realised, is dropping down deep into the ground of his being, so to say. This seed may disappear below ground for a long while, and maybe he will think that it has died, but one day he will look with unbelieving eyes on the first shoot pushing up above the surface of his conscious mind. Unless he takes this statement on faith, his mind will become restless at this stage and it will wonder what it should be doing, and what is going to happen next. Nothing will happen immediately, just as nothing outwardly happens immediately when the sower lets the seed fall into the ground; but provided that the pupil does not allow the ground of his mind to grow rank, results will appear in due time.

We will try to describe what we have been told takes place after these three stages, when the meditator is rising in his art; for to talk of the end of an ascent encourages a climber. There comes a point, early or late—it differs with the temperament and maturity of the meditator—when the inner scrutiny we have tried to describe is withdrawn, and is succeeded by a conscious recognition of identity with the subject of meditation. This change is not engineered by the will or the mind; it is brought about by the life and reality residing in the subject of meditation itself, which communicates itself to the meditator when the channel between them is clear. There is a world of difference between the last moment when the activity springs from the meditator and the first moment when it is revealed as residing in the subject upon which he has been exerting his powers, up to this time. One might almost say that he ceases to draw towards the meditation, and that the truth in the meditation now approaches him.

To use a simile which has only a flash of truth in it, but which may be useful as an indication of the state—the higher meditation may be likened to a bird sitting on her eggs; before those eggs are there, she sits for a long time among the branches, singing and looking down into the tree in which her nest is to be made. She is there of her own choice; but once the nest has been made and the eggs laid, she has no choice, they draw her, and she descends upon them and broods them. It is the life in the eggs which now infuses her with alertness and the sense of identity, and due to the warmth and protection of her continuous presence the life in them reveals itself to her in due course.

We are taught that this higher stage of meditation is a fusion, a revelation and a self-obliterating experience; but it is only reached by patient application—that is, patient building and continuous brooding.

Marjorie Waterhouse has written elsewhere: 'Identification in love is the final secret and not the learning, training and purification, although these have an essential and refining function to perform'. 'Identification in love is the final secret'—we should ponder on these words. It explains why the Teachers of meditation lay stress on *feeling* the meditation and why many meditation texts include a devotional element in them. We will repeat now one such practice which we have done before. I will read again the words of Marjorie Waterhouse:

Remind yourself again and again that, as the Lord is omnipresent, you are doing this meditation in His presence. The meditation is: 'Show Thy Face to me. Make me worthy of Thy love, O Love Supreme, O Beauty Absolute'. This is a prayer to the Unconditioned, asking that It may become conditioned. When you have repeated it a few times, then gather up the central meaning in your heart as, so to say, 'reveal, reveal!' and feel and contemplate it there. Then wait, in a quiescent receptive state—not for a vision of that Face but for a sense of its reality and immanence.

OM

Show Thy Face to me. Make me worthy of Thy Love, O Love Supreme, O Beauty Absolute.

OM

Psychologically the progressive stages of meditation may be said to be 'I know it', 'I feel it' and 'I am it'. (Students of Vedanta may question whether this is an accurate description of shravana, manana and nididhyasana, but for our purposes it suffices). It is this third stage which is termed 'Self-identification'. There is a Sufi tradition that a disciple came to the house of the Teacher Bayazid when he was meditating and called out through the front door: 'Is Bayazid at home?' Back came the call from inside the house: 'Is there anyone here but God?'

Consider now the well-known haiku of the Japanese poet Basho, who was also a great mystic:

61

Old pond.
A frog jumps in.
Plop!

So much in a few syllables! What does it mean? It is the picture of a meditator, and if you see a frog sitting motionless in the garden or beside a pond, it is not unlike someone sitting in meditation. The frog is quite motionless, yet balanced and alert. At a certain moment he jumps into the pond: it is a very old pond. It means that the individualized ego-consciousness, which has been functioning in the mud of duality and the grass of separateness and distinctions, jumps into the beginning-less Absolute, into the One Reality, into OM OM OM. Where is the individuality of the frog now? It has vanished in self-identification with the One Reality. All that remains behind is the 'plop' of the vibrations of his meditations which are felt by those who are still in the mud and grass of duality.

We will now repeat a previous practice and meditate for five minutes on 'I sit in the direct light and stillness of Thy being', trying to feel merged and identified with that light:

OM

I sit in the direct light and stillness of Thy being.

OM

This is perhaps a good moment to remind you of the practice which Marjorie Waterhouse recommended should be done during the day:

Meditating Frog

Remember that you are performing action and under-going all experience in the invisible presence of the Lord, and look upon all that comes as a message from Him to you, and on your reaction to it as an offering from you to Him. Do not try to do this all day because, if you do, you will probably pass judgment against it and forget all about it. Do it for, say, half an hour at a time and repeat the practice at definite times during the day.

Let us not forget that our meditations are an offering to the Lord and are for the good of all—not only to benefit ourselves. So, as our last practice today, let us meditate for a few minutes on:

OM

May all derive good from me.
May I derive good from all.

OM

The concluding poem is by our Teacher, Hari Prasad Shastri:

I saw a beautiful sunset, golden, purple and silvery.
It painted doors and palaces and invited my soul to enter.
'How can I go without my friends
Who have walked through the woods and hills with me?'
I said to myself—and looked round for them.
The sunset vanished.
My soul revealed to me a dawn of eternal light and peace.

WEEK 6: The Canvas of Meditation

Reverence to Hari Prasad Shastri!

This is the final session of the six-week course during which we have analyzed the science of meditation under its main aspects, from the beginnings of stilling the mind and bringing it under control to the culmination of identification with Self, which is known as samadhi in Yoga. Today we will look at meditation as a whole, and together do several practices, some familiar, some new. First we will do a short visualization practice on OM.

The importance of creating a focus within us which will claim our love and service was the subject of the fourth session of this course. Some like to use as a focus a personalized form of the One Reality—the form of Christ or Krishna or Buddha—but not all want to or can. Our Teacher said that *everyone* can use OM, which is a symbol of all that is highest and most beautiful. He has written: 'All that is holiest and best in inspired literature, all that has ever been said or will be said to prepare man to have a right relationship with Reality or God, is summed up in OM'. This practice, which he has given, is simple but powerful. The method is to look at the symbol OM in relaxation for two minutes with the eyes open. After that, close your eyes and dwell on it in imagination for three minutes. I will repeat the method once more and we will do it:

OM

Look at OM in relaxation for two minutes with the eyes open.

OM

65

The Symbol OM

OM

*Close your eyes and dwell on OM in imagination
for three minutes.*

OM

A short description of the whole process of meditation is given in Shanti Sadan's publication *Freedom through Self-Realisation*:

In the early stages the practice of meditation is a matter of the application of the will to control and direct the mind in the way in which it is desired to go. Later, the higher meditation transcends this stage and the will is no longer the controller. But that is the stage only attained after considerable mastery in Yoga.

In St Teresa's famous simile, the garden of the soul has in the first stage of prayer to be watered by laboriously lifting the water from a well, a process requiring much effort and bringing little reward in return. But as progress is made and the second stage of prayer is entered, the watering process becomes like that to be found in the Spain of her time, where the water was often raised by a string of many buckets mounted on a wheel. Effort is still needed to raise it, but it is very much more effective. A much greater volume of water is raised for the same expenditure of will-power, time and energy. This is the stage, says St Teresa, when the soul begins to be recollected, in other words when some degree of control and restraint of the mind has been achieved by the earlier practice.

In a yet more advanced stage of meditation, which

St Teresa calls the third degree of prayer, the watering process becomes analogous, she says, to the watering of the garden by a stream. Here the stream flows spontaneously and continuously and the only effort needed from the will is to direct the water towards the part of the garden which it is desired to cultivate. The will is becoming less important and the process easier, because of the degree of mastery of the mind which the individual has attained. And the culmination of the meditation process is in that fourth stage of prayer of which St Teresa speaks, where the garden is watered by the downpour of rain. It is the most effective way of watering the garden and the one which most clearly ensures its fertility and prosperity, and it is completely independent of the will of the meditator.

This is the state of the illumined mind, receiving its spiritual light and nourishment from the Lord Himself, seated within the mind. This is the state which in Yoga is called samadhi.

Samadhi in Yoga is not, then, as some people wrongly imagine, a trance-like state of oblivion which comes and goes. It is the state of the illumined mind in which it receives without intermission, and no matter what it is engaged upon, spiritual light and nourishment and inspiration from the Lord seated within the mind. It is a permanent condition which is as much present in the hurly-burly of daily life as it is in the seclusion of a retreat. Brother Lawrence, who knew about it, wrote: 'The time of business does not with me differ from the time of prayer; and in the noise and clatter of my kitchen, while several persons are at the same time calling for different things, I possess God in as great tranquillity as if I were upon my knees at the blessed sacrament'. It is to this state of Grace and illumination that the meditator aspires.

An important point, not to be lost sight of, is that the process of meditation is not to create anything new; its purpose is only to remove obstructions so that the background of the real Self (Atman), against which all our experiences are played out, may emerge as the dominant feature of our lives.

You will find in an issue of our journal *Self-Knowledge* (Volume 39 No.2) a meditation text of our Teacher: 'Paint thy pictures, O mind, but the canvas, colour and light is my Self, is my Self, is my Self'. Let us try it for a few minutes. The method given is as follows:

Sit in relaxation. Withdraw the mind inwards from the sense-objects. Repeat the text to yourself a few times: 'OM. Paint thy pictures, O mind, but the canvas, colour and light is my Self, is my Self, is my Self. OM'. Let the mind paint whatever pictures it wishes; it does not matter. Whatever pictures come up in the mind, just sit and enjoy them as if you were watching a show on television; and all the time keep remembering 'the canvas, colour and light is my Self, is my Self, is my Self'. Let the mind paint its own pictures. Don't interfere with it. Just watch the pictures and sense underneath the current of joy, serenity and inner peace which is my Self, is my Self, is my Self.

OM

Paint thy pictures, O mind, but the canvas,
colour and light is my Self, is my Self, is my Self.

OM

There is a story of a Zen abbot who said to one of the young monks: 'Bring me a clean bowl'. The monk spent some time assiduously cleaning and polishing a bowl before bringing it back to the abbot, who greeted him with the words: 'Now put it back where you found it'. The story illustrates the process of meditation. The mind is like a bowl which has first to be located and then made clean and emptied of all its rubbishy contents. This is the first phase of meditation—and one that can last a long time—when the will-power and effort and sincerity of the seeker are put to the test. (The first two sessions of this course dealt with this phase). When progress in meditation has led to the creation of an internal focus other than the ego, the mind begins to take second place to the Self (Atman) and ultimately can be put away and forgotten about. The great Chinese Yogi Wang Yang Ming made the creation of the focus one of the main planks of his teaching. He called the background canvas of the One Reality 'Tien-Li' (literally 'the Heaven-given Principle') and he says: 'It is simply a question of keeping the Heaven-given Principle in mind, for this in itself is what it means by "creating the focus". If one is able to remember the focus, it will become gradually fixed in the mind. One who constantly harbours a regard for the Heaven-given Principle, little by little becomes a glorious great Sage and a God-man. But it is also necessary, in obedience to the thought, to nurture and practise moral principles'.

That which Wang Yang Ming called 'the Heaven-given Principle' the yogis call the Self (Atman) or the One Reality. It is symbolized by OM. So let us for the next practice meditate for five minutes on the text, already known to us:

OM

There is but one reality. OM! OM! OM!

OM

Marjorie Waterhouse gave us a gift beyond price in the practice which we have been doing each week: 'I sit in the direct light and stillness of Thy being'. This is a practice of the Presence of God and its unique value lies in its flexibility. If you take nothing else away from this course, it is to be hoped that you will make use of this one practice. It is all-purpose and useful at every stage of the meditation process. Early on it can be used to create silence in the mind because it reminds us of the *stillness* of the Self and its calming influence. In fact, when she first mentioned it, Marjorie Waterhouse gave it as a practice 'useful to withstand the assaults of the mind'. Later, it helps to create the focus because, as Wang Yang Ming says, 'creating the focus' means nothing other than keeping in the mind without interruption the awareness of the *direct light and stillness of being*.

It can be used as the chosen text at the fixed time of meditation, and it can also be adapted to link up with the practice to be done during the day: ('Remember that

one of these magmatic 2-
formulas to ___

29 CHEPSTOW VILLAS.
W. 11.

TELEPHONE
PARK 7341

" I sleep (or talk, or work —
— whatever you are doing)
in the direct light or stillness
of (Thy) being" Sometimes it
will include 'Thy' sometimes
'being' only. The result of
this is that slowly you become
more aware of this descent
+ interpenetration, than of
what is going on in the
mind, + in fact less + less
goes on in the mind unto

Original Manuscript of the Practice

72

that influence: this belief
has got to be constantly fostered
at first, afterwards it will
be accepted, support &
influence the mind.
Another even more simple
formula, & yet I get benefit
from it is — "These are the
murmurs of the separative
life" or when thoughts
arise, & that you are aware
that they are arising, which
in fact, often are not —
& 'Thou art not there, thou
art here' This creates a

given by Marjorie Waterhouse

you are performing action and undergoing all experience in the invisible presence of the Lord, and look upon all that comes as a message from Him to you, and on your reaction to it as an offering from you to Him'.) The way to remember that you are performing action and undergoing all experience in the invisible presence of the Lord is to change the verb 'sit' in this text to any other verb which is appropriate to what you are doing. Thus, if you are eating at the time, you remember 'I am eating in the direct light and stillness of Thy being'. If you are shopping, you remember 'I am shopping in the direct light and stillness of Thy being' and so forth. This is the way this formula can be used to activate the practice of remembrance during the day.

We will use it now as a chosen meditation text and, since we are sitting at the moment, we will retain the wording 'I sit in the direct light and stillness of Thy being'. I will repeat the text once again and we will feel it as vividly as we can for the next five minutes:

OM

I sit in the direct light and stillness of Thy being.

OM

Our Teacher has said: 'Everything has to remind us of the meditation'. The practices at a fixed time are only the beginning of the attempt to feel *the direct light and stillness of being* continuously, all the time, whatever we are doing. In the short paragraph which will now be read, our Teacher indicates the sort of way we can try to refer even sense-experiences to the background canvas of the Supreme Self:

> To enjoy the beauty of an infant or a flower, you must merge your mind in the same mass-Consciousness which is common to both the subject and the object. Do not stand away from an object of nature, a flower or a man. Beauty is not in the form but in the meaning it expresses. Lift up yourself and the object of your love to a super-world, and there enjoy it. Not in the ceaseless motion which is on the surface but in the eternal tranquillity which is its nature, abides the idea of beauty. The real enjoyment of a flower is in living with it, in it, above the tranquillity and identity.

It is admittedly a difficult line of thought, and for most of us it may be easier during the day, whenever we can, to bring to mind and remember, whatever we are experiencing at the moment: 'I am having this experience in the direct light and stillness of Thy being'. And at the fixed time of meditation, we can also use this as our chosen text, as we have been doing during these six weeks.

On one occasion our Teacher said: 'If you want to change the world, meditate! Social service is good but if, instead of the mania of doing service to somebody, a hundred people devoted themselves to the contemplation of God day and night, they would create new waves in the spiritual aether'. So those who have the good of everybody at heart can do most good to them by learning to meditate. And in fact meditation should always be done for the good of all and not only to benefit ourselves.

So, as our last practice today we will meditate again on the text which is said to open the heart to the universality of Consciousness or God, and the consequent oneness of all:

OM

May all derive good from me.
May I derive good from all.

OM

We have already listened to one account in prose of the process of meditation so, to conclude, let us hear a poetical account given by Dr Shastri in his verses entitled 'Samadhi':

It is a dark and stormy night.
The wind is howling like a pack of wolves.
Snow is falling like the sighs of a young widow
Over the death of her only child.

I sit in a small hut, dark and solitary.
The cedar branches, tossed by the wind,
Sweep the ice from the roof.
They are like the consoling words of Dada
Administering relief during a cholera epidemic.

I have lighted my only candle in my dark chamber.
I am waiting for Thy promised visit.
My hope flickers and burns with the flame.
The candle is being consumed—and I wait.

Every rustle of the wind appears to be Thy
    footstep.
Every turning of the branches appears to announce
    Thy approach.
The flame of the candle almost touches the sand
    on which it stands.
My sighs grow deeper; yet my soul is lit with hope.
I wait and I wait and I wait.

A gust of wind blows out the dying flame.
All is dark within and without.

Another flame is suddenly lit in my soul.
Thou hast come! Thou hast come!
The night, the dark, the loneliness, are turned to
    light and bliss.
The hut gives way before the shock of the storm.
The winds are Thy kisses,
The darkness Thy mantle, revealing Thy moonlit
    face.

The wolves are singing odes of my union with
    Thee.
Heaven and earth have departed. Time has slipped
    away.
Even my own existence is blotted out.
The stream has reached the sea, the dreamless
    sleep of Turiya.
All is Rama, Rama, Rama.

Hari Prasad Shastri gave the progressive stages of Adhyatma Yoga as (1) Withdraw (2) Focus, and (3) Be unified with the light within. The practice of meditation will accompany each of these stages and, in the process, will itself be experienced as deepening and progressing but... there are no short cuts! Thus, withdrawal at will from sense-objects and from reflection upon them must have been achieved to a marked degree before the focus can be established, which is the crucial breakthrough in step (2).

The flexible practice suggested by Marjorie Waterhouse (page 71) will be found useful at any and every stage. It is something of a puzzle that her original formula, which is intended to be capable of applying to the whole gamut of human activities, should begin with the words 'I sleep... in the direct light and stillness of (Thy) being'. Could it have been chosen because we spend as much as one-third of our life in sleep, or is there a hint here that we are spiritually asleep and that this practice can awaken us to the focussed life?